PUPPY CARE AND CRITTERS, TOO!

Judy Petersen-Fleming
and Bill Fleming

Photographs by Debra Reingold-Reiss

Tambourine Books
New York

This book is dedicated to all the people who devote their lives to the care and well-being of animals. It's also for all those children who will grow up to choose lifestyles and careers and do the same.

ACKNOWLEDGMENTS

Our most sincere appreciation to the institutions that supplied the critter photographs. We applaud their commitment to educating the public about the animals and their habitats that we call the wild kingdom.

At Marine World Africa U.S.A., Vallejo, California, special thanks to Mary O'Herron, Darryl Bush, and Jim Bonde, who have been extraordinary to work with, and to the devoted people that care for their animals: Steve Nagle, Kim Broadfoot, Lori Hill, Mark Jardarian, J.R., Karen Povey, and Lynn Myers.

At San Diego Zoo, San Diego, California, very special thanks to Jeff Jouett and Laurie Krusinski for all their help and to a dedicated keeper, Vickie Kuder.

At Sea World, Orlando, Florida, we'd like to acknowledge Jack Pearson and Toni Caracciolo for all the time and help they gave us, as well as animal care specialist Pat Caracciolo.

At Sea World, San Diego, California, thanks to Margaret Retzlaff for her patience and ready help at any given time, and to the people whose care for the animals is reflected in the pictures throughout this book: Julie Scardina-Ludwig, Eric Bogden, and Kevin Robinson.

Special thanks to renowned veterinarian Kevin T. Fitzgerald, D.V.M.

Thanks also to all the organizations whose mission is to find homes for orphaned animals, some of whom are featured throughout this book: Animal Orphanage, Colorado Humane Society and SPCA, The Cat Care Society, Denver Dumb Friends League—Humane Society of Denver, Inc., Intermountain Humane Society, Max Fund Adoption Center, and Save An Animal Foundation.

NOTE TO PARENTS:

Raising a puppy can be a wonderful experience for a child as well as the whole family. Whether you read to your son or daughter, or your child  reads to younger siblings, the easy-care methods described in this book will help your children feel pride in caring for their pet.

The keepers and trainers of the exotic animals feel the same way, as you will discover throughout this book. It's never too soon to teach our children respect for animals—whether they are the ones we keep at home or the ones we visit in zoos and marine parks. While providing love and proper care to a pet, children will begin to understand and appreciate all animals much more.

When your family is ready to choose a new companion, don't forget to go to the local animal shelter first. The many orphaned dogs and puppies make the best pets!

Now that you have decided to bring a puppy home you will want to know how to take care of it. There are a few important things to learn that will keep your new puppy healthy and make him a happy member of your family.

Throughout this book you will also see the keepers and trainers in wild animal parks taking care of their animals. They are doing just what you are learning to do.

Don't forget that a happy, healthy pet is fun to have around.

A PUPPY SHOULD NOT BE SEPARATED FROM ITS MOTHER FOR AT LEAST SEVEN WEEKS.

When you go to choose your puppy from the pound or a litter, watch each one carefully. Which puppy is curious and wags his tail? Which ones are shy and trying to hide?

Pick a friendly puppy. Clap your hands or walk away. The puppy who comes to you is the one who wants to be friendly.

Just like your new puppy, each one of these young dolphins has its own personality. Some are very active and playful, while others can be very shy so it takes longer for the trainer to get to know them.

DOLPHINS CAN SWIM AT SPEEDS UP TO THIRTY MILES PER HOUR.

YOU CAN TELL YOUR PUPPY IS
AFRAID WHEN HE PULLS HIS
TAIL DOWN BETWEEN HIS LEGS
AND HUNCHES LOW TO
THE GROUND.

The first day in your puppy's new home can be very tiring for her and sometimes scary, too. You or another family member should let the puppy spend the first few nights in the bedroom.

Put a blanket or piece of carpet on the floor next to your bed, but don't worry if she decides to pick her own spot. You may want to lie with your puppy for a few minutes to help her settle down.

After such a big day, she will probably sleep through the night, but if she wakes up, a soothing pat should calm her down.

KING PENGUIN CHICKS ARE BROWN AND DO NOT GROW INTO THEIR BEAUTIFUL BLACK AND WHITE SUITS UNTIL THEY ARE FOUR MONTHS OLD. THEY CAN GROW UP TO THREE FEET TALL.

These young penguins have been in their new home for less than twenty-four hours. Their keepers stayed with them all night, feeding them every three or four hours and making sure that the larger chicks did not pick on the smaller ones.

The penguin keepers will stay with these chicks around-the-clock for the first couple of days to see that they are comfortable and are eating well.

DOGS ARE SOCIAL ANIMALS, LIKE DOLPHINS, ELEPHANTS, AND CHIMPANZEES.

Puppies take time! The first three months of your puppy's life are the most important for you and your family. He needs lots of attention during this stage.

A dog is a social animal. If he were a wild dog he would spend all of his time with his pack. But in your home it is you and your family who will become his friends.

After school and before you go out to play, it is important to give your puppy a lot of time and attention. This may mean you might have to take time from other activities.

AND CRITTERS, TOO!

This keeper knows how important it is to spend a lot of time with baby koala Caloola. She talks and soothes Caloola as she's being weighed and puts her favorite stuffed toy in the scale with her. Spending this time with Caloola now will make her feel secure and happy as she grows up.

KOALAS ARE NOT RELATED TO BEARS. THEY ARE RELATED TO KANGAROOS AND ALSO CARRY THEIR YOUNG IN POUCHES.

PUPPIES ARE BORN WITH THEIR PUPPY TEETH. THEY LOSE THESE TEETH BEGINNING AT THREE MONTHS AND WILL HAVE ALL THEIR ADULT TEETH BY SIX MONTHS.

Your puppy will depend on you to make sure she is cared for and fed daily. You can also share this job with your brother or sister so they can feel part of caring for your puppy, too.

Younger brothers or sisters can help you by pouring the dry food into the bowl. Parents can help you decide what kind of food your puppy needs and how much.

AND CRITTERS, TOO!

MANATEE CALVES CAN WEIGH UP TO SIXTY POUNDS WHEN THEY ARE BORN.

When this orphaned baby manatee, Little Joe, was first rescued, his trainers had to take extra care to make sure he was getting the best diet to help him grow properly. Since a manatee's diet is so special, the keepers rely on the vet to help them.

PUPPIES AND DOGS PANT TO
COOL THEMSELVES OFF — THEY
BREATHE HARD WITH THEIR
TONGUES OUT.

Puppies need to drink water several times a day. It can be dangerous to your puppy's health if he ever gets thirsty for a long period of time. You can be sure he is getting enough water by always making it available for him.

Place a full bowl of water near the area where your puppy eats and keep a full bowl outside too. Sometimes try giving him a drink from a garden hose after a play session or long walk.

14

IN THE WILD, KOALAS GET MOST OF THEIR WATER FROM EUCALYPTUS LEAVES. THESE LEAVES ARE THE ONLY FOOD THAT KOALAS EAT.

This keeper knows how important it is to make sure Gumdrop always has water to drink. Gumdrop needs water so she won't overheat and get sick.

A DOG HAS VERY GOOD EARS AND CAN HEAR A WHISTLE SO HIGH IN PITCH, YOU WILL NOT BE ABLE TO HEAR IT AT ALL!

House-training your puppy to go the bathroom outside is your job. To start house-training, take her out immediately after she eats, after playtime, when she wakes up from a nap, and before bedtime.

Take her to the same outdoor spot each time and stand around and wait. If she comes in without going potty, keep taking her out every ten minutes until she goes.

Every time your puppy goes to the bathroom in the right spot give her lots of love and praise. This teaches her that she has done what is right and will also help her to remember to always potty outside.

ORANGUTANS COME FROM INDONESIA. THE WORD ORANGUTAN MEANS "OLD MAN OF THE FOREST."

To help keep her home clean, this baby orangutan, Kayla, learned to wear diapers when she was very young. Her trainer had to teach her to keep the diapers on and to not rip them off.

When Kayla finally learned to leave the diapers on, the trainer gave her lots of love and praise so she'd know she'd done right — exactly like you do with your puppy.

ALL DOGS ARE TERRITORIAL, WHICH MEANS THEY PROTECT THE AREA IN WHICH THEY LIVE.

Poop patrol needs to be done daily in your backyard. All you need is a shovel and a paper bag to pick up after your puppy. It's easy if you do it everyday. Then you and your puppy will have a cleaner and safer place to play.

If you live in an apartment, bring a small plastic bag and paper sack with you when you take your puppy outside. After your puppy goes potty, place the plastic bag around it and scoop it into a small paper bag. Throw the bag in the garbage as soon as you get back to your apartment.

Accidents do happen. If you catch your puppy going potty inside, say a stern "no" and take him outside. Never spank your puppy. Spanking doesn't work with puppies and can actually do more harm than good.

This trainer takes great pride in cleaning up the large area in which these rhinos, Ma and Pa, live. Ma and Pa are much happier when their home is nice and clean.

RHINO HORNS ARE NOT HORNS AT ALL, BUT THOUSANDS OF HAIRS PRESSED TOGETHER.

PUPPIES CAN MAKE UP THEIR OWN PLAY GAMES, SUCH AS CHASING THEIR TAILS.

Playtime is very important for your puppy. It helps him keep fit, alert, and happy.

Playing with your puppy can be lots of fun for you both. Puppies love to play at running and chasing, hide-and-seek, and tug-of-war.

Play a game that will help your puppy learn his name. Have your family or friends stand in different spots in the yard or park. Take turns calling the puppy. Each time he comes when he is called give him lots of praise.

CHIMPANZEES ARE TICKLISH, JUST LIKE PEOPLE.

This baby chimpanzee, Maggie, really enjoys playing with her trainer. They play chase and hide-and-seek. Maggie also loves to imitate her. Because they spend so much time playing, they have become very good friends. Just like you and your puppy will!

ALL DOGS HAVE FORTY-TWO
TEETH. FOUR OF THEM ARE
FANG-LIKE CANINES.

Toys can make playtime even more fun! Almost anything can be a toy for a puppy. But before you give her a toy, always make sure there is nothing sharp on it and that small pieces can't break off and get swallowed.

Pieces of hard leather, old rags, balls, and squeaky toys are just some toys to try. Any toy made out of rawhide is a good choice because it satisfies the puppy's need to chew.

Don't forget natural toys like sticks and large twigs, which can entertain your puppy for hours.

AND CRITTERS, TOO!

Sea lions love to play! Priscilla, a young sea lion, loves to push around her favorite ball.

Priscilla's trainer gives her different toys every day so she won't get bored playing with the same one.

SEA LIONS ACTUALLY MAKE A BARKING SOUND LIKE A DOG.

A GROWING PUPPY WILL SLEEP EIGHTEEN TO TWENTY HOURS A DAY.

Puppies will need daily naps while they are growing. You need to be careful that you don't over tire your pup, so let him rest when he needs it. He will learn to feel secure and comfortable next to you during this time. Sharing quiet time together will also make the two of you better friends.

AND CRITTERS, TOO!

Shamu is very active but still needs his rest, just like your puppy. This trainer will spend time in the water just relaxing with Shamu. They have become better friends because Shamu knows that the two of them can rest and relax together.

KILLER WHALES CAN GROW UP TO THIRTY-ONE FEET LONG AND WEIGH UP TO EIGHTEEN THOUSAND POUNDS!

A MOTHER DOG WILL SNUGGLE UP TO HER PUPPIES TO GIVE THEM WARMTH AND COMFORT.

Your puppy will enjoy all the time you take to hug and pet him. You need to be careful that your hugs are very gentle, especially when the puppy is young.

During petting time, always make very slow, gentle movements with your hands. Fast hands can excite and confuse your puppy, making him think it is playtime instead of quiet time.

AND CRITTERS, TOO!

IN THE WILD, RIVER OTTERS LIVE IN SMALL FAMILY GROUPS AND FEED ON FISH.

This river otter enjoys the hugs his trainer gives him each day. The trainer also knows to use a slow, gentle hand when petting so the young otter doesn't become excited or confused.

The trainer spent one year just watching the care the other trainers gave to all the otters. Now that he knows how to gently handle an otter, all the other otters feel very comfortable with him.

ALL DOGS AND PUPPIES HAVE
FUR COATS. SOME ARE
LONG AND SOME ARE SHORT;
SOME HAVE SOFT FUR
AND SOME HAVE COARSE FUR.
A FUR COAT PROTECTS
THEM AND KEEPS
THEM WARM.

It will also be your job to help teach your younger brother or sister to be gentle with the new puppy. You set an example by showing how softly you handle your puppy. When they see how gentle you are, they will be able to copy you.

These trainers all work together while teaching the baby tigers to stay in their "Tiger Taxis." They teach them to ride in these buggies so they can be taken to play in the grass or even to the kid's playground!

TIGER CUBS ONLY WEIGH TWO TO THREE POUNDS WHEN THEY ARE BORN, BUT CAN GROW UP TO WEIGH OVER FIVE HUNDRED POUNDS.

DOGS ARE DISTANT RELATIVES
OF THE WOLF. WOLVES
KEEP ORDER IN THEIR PACK BY
USING EYE CONTACT.

When you first start spending time with your puppy you should always keep eye contact with him. This will help him pay attention to what you are saying and doing. It will also help you as you start training your puppy.

AND CRITTERS, TOO!

This trainer is starting to teach the baby walrus to swim with him and play games in the water. The trainer always keeps eye contact so the baby walrus will trust him and know what to do.

A WALRUS HAS OVER ONE HUNDRED WHISKERS THAT ARE MADE OF THE SAME MATERIAL AS YOUR FINGERNAILS. THEY USE THE WHISKERS LIKE FINGERS TO MOVE FOOD TO THEIR MOUTHS.

THE AVERAGE DOG CAN UNDERSTAND THIRTY-FIVE TO FORTY-FIVE WORDS.

This girl is teaching her puppy not to run out the front door. She is telling her "no." You need to start teaching your puppy "no" right away. Whenever your puppy is doing something you don't want her to, say a stern "no" to her. Always use the same word and the same tone of voice. It will confuse your puppy if you say other words like "stop" or "don't." And you should never yell "no." This will only frighten your puppy, and she cannot learn if she is afraid.

This trainer is telling the baby cheetah "no" after she playfully tried to take a nip at him.

Mara learned the meaning of "no" when she was very young. Sometimes Mara forgets. Then the trainer gently reminds her what "no" means.

CHEETAHS ARE THE FASTEST LAND ANIMAL IN THE WORLD. THEY CAN RUN AT SPEEDS OVER SIXTY MILES PER HOUR.

THE FASTEST DOG IN THE
WORLD IS A GREYHOUND,
WHICH CAN RUN AT SPEEDS OF
UP TO FORTY MILES PER HOUR.

You can train your puppy to do many things. You can teach him to walk on a leash so the two of you can go places together. You can teach him to "sit" and to "come." Remember to always use the same word to teach a new command, just like you do when saying "no."

Take your time with your puppy when you're training him. Remember to give a lot of praise and love when he does the right thing.

COUGARS CAN JUMP HIGHER THAN ANY OTHER ANIMAL IN THE WORLD. THEY CAN JUMP EIGHTEEN TO TWENTY FEET STRAIGHT UP IN THE AIR!

These trainers taught both the baby cougar, Sequoia, and the baby white tiger, Rajah, to walk on a leash. Since they spend so much time with Sequoia and Rajah, it was easy for them to train these young cats. Now they can go explore the park and try climbing up trees.

YOU CAN TELL YOUR PUPPY
IS HAPPY WHEN HE WAGS
HIS TAIL QUICKLY.

All the time and care you give
your puppy will make him very
happy to live with his family.
You have a friend for life!

36

WHERE TO VISIT THE KEEPERS AND THEIR ANIMALS

p. 7

p. 31

SEA WORLD OF CALIFORNIA

1720 SOUTH SHORES ROAD

SAN DIEGO, CA 92109

FOR INFORMATION CALL:

(619) 226-3901

p. 25

SEA WORLD OF FLORIDA

7007 SEA WORLD DRIVE

ORLANDO, FL 32821

FOR INFORMATION CALL:

(407) 363-2613

p. 9

p. 13

p. 27

MARINE WORLD AFRICA U.S.A.

MARINE WORLD PARKWAY

VALLEJO, CA 94589

FOR INFORMATION CALL:

(707) 644-4000

p. 17   p. 19   p. 21

p. 23   p. 29   p. 33   p. 35

SAN DIEGO ZOO

2920 ZOO DRIVE

SAN DIEGO, CA 92109

FOR INFORMATION CALL:

(619) 234-3153

p. 11   p. 15

Library of Congress Cataloging in Publication Data
Petersen-Fleming, Judy. Puppy care and critters, too!/by Judy Petersen-Fleming and Bill Fleming; photographs by
Debra Reingold-Reiss. —1st ed. p. cm. Summary: Photographs and text describe how to choose and care for a pet
puppy. Comparisons are made with the care and behavior of wild animals in zoos and wild animal parks.
1. Puppies—Juvenile literature. 2. Animals—Juvenile literature. [1. Dogs. 2. Animals.
3. Pets.] I. Fleming, Bill. II. Reingold-Reiss, Debra, ill. III. Title
SF426.5.P45 1994 636.7'07—dc20 93-23129 CIP AC
ISBN 0-688-12563-8 (trade). — ISBN 0-688-12564-6 (lib. bdg.)
1 3 5 7 9 10 8 6 4 2
First edition

PHOTO CREDITS
Cover photographs by Darryl Bush/Marine World Africa U.S.A., Vallejo, California.
Photographs on pages 7, 25, and 31, copyright © 1994 by Sea World of California.
Photographs on pages 9, 13, and 27, copyright © 1994 by Sea World of Florida.
Photographs on pages 11 and 15 copyright © 1994 by the Zoological Society of San Diego.
Photographs on pages 17, 19, 21, 23, 29, 33, and 35 by Darryl Bush copyright © 1994 by
Marine World Africa U.S.A., Vallejo, California.